GOD CREATED

Some Thoughts About
The Awesome World Around Us
And God Who Created It All

BY GEORGE L. HERLEIN

INTRODUCTION

*W*hen people think about the question "Where did this world come from?" a variety of responses come forth. Some may respond that it's always been here, while others may say it is the result of a big explosion. But I hope you are one who responds with the understanding that God created it. We don't usually spend much time, however, thinking about the actual processes involved in the creation of all that surrounds us. Many of the details are open only to speculation. But the more we examine God's Word the more we find about creation: past, present and future. I hope some of the thoughts expressed in this devotional will help you to contemplate the awesome universe around us and God who made it all. Having been a Christian for most of my eighty-four years, and having studied the Bible for much of that time, I have had the privilege of teaching Sunday school classes for adults and of leading small group Bible studies. I have been a member of two Baptist churches during the past fifty years where God's Word has been taught in Sunday services, weekly Bible study classes, prayer meetings and Sunday School classes. I have recently become aware that, when it comes to creation, we are often satisfied to accept "God created the heavens and the earth" and to give the process no further thought. As I have been led to contemplate what was involved I began writing some of my thoughts, first only for my own benefit. Later I was encouraged by Pastor George Johnson to try my hand for the first time at putting them into a form that could be passed on to others. I pray that these thoughts will be as much of a blessing to the reader as they have been to me.

ACKNOWLEDGMENTS

Thanks to Pastor George Johnson of Hope Community Baptist Church, Sterling Heights, Michigan, (hope4macomb.com), whose encouragement has caused what started as a bit of personal writing to become published for others. Thanks also to others who gave an encouraging word after having read all or part of it.

TABLE OF CONTENTS

1

IN THE BEGINNING

he Word of God opens with the declaration, "In the beginning God created the heavens and the earth. The earth was without form and void; and darkness was on the face of the deep. And the Spirit of God was hovering over the face of the waters" (Genesis 1:1-2). No explanation is given of who God is, what is meant by the beginning, of what the heavens and earth consist or what it means to create.

Then, through the first two chapters of Genesis, we begin to get some ideas about what was involved:

- At first the earth was without form and was void (empty?).
- Darkness was on the face of the deep.
- The Spirit of God was over the face of the waters.

We are told water covers a dark, formless something and God is, or has, a Spirit that is present.

In Genesis 1:21 we learn more about creation: God "created" sea creatures and every living thing that moves in the water and all the winged birds, in each case, "according to its kind." And God saw these things were good. The next use of "created" is in Genesis 1:27. God created man in His own image, and man was created as both male and female. The last use of the word "created" in these first two chapters of Genesis is in chapter 2, verse 4: "This is the history of the heavens and the earth when they were created in the day that the Lord God made the earth and the heavens."

One of the descriptive words used, as we see more in His Word, is "made." We have some experience with that because we make things also. As we take material that is available and put it together, so it becomes something useful. In Genesis 1:16 we read that God made two great lights, and He made the stars. He made the beast of the earth and cattle and everything that creeps on the earth, each according to its kind (1:25). It appears that "made" and "created" are the same, since both are used to describe the making of the heavens and the earth (2:4). He made every tree grow that is good for food (2:9), and He made a rib into a woman (2:22).

In Genesis 1:2-3 we are told that darkness was on the face of the deep. But God said, "Let there be light," and there was light. He then divided the light from the darkness. Many other acts of creation were in response to the words "Let there be": "Let there be a firmament in the midst of the waters" (1:6). This is followed in the next verse by "God made the firmament." So there seems to be little difference in how things are brought about. The word "firmament" is variously translated "heaven" or "sky" in common versions of the Bible. Verse 7 continues: "God divided the waters which were under the firmament from the waters above the firmament." Next He said, "Let the waters be gathered together in one place and let the dry land appear," and it was so (1:9).

Following that, God called forth grass, herbs, fruit trees, fruit and seeds, all according to their kind (1:11). The filling of the earth and skies with all kinds of good things had begun. In Genesis 1:14-19 we notice a combination of "Let there be" and "made." First He spoke into existence lights that would divide night from day and tell seasons, days and years, and then He made two great lights, one for day and the other for night. Again, we see a combination: He said let the waters be filled with living creatures and let the birds fly across the firmament (1:20-22). That is followed by: God created sea creatures and all things in the waters and winged birds, and He spoke the words telling them to be fruitful and multiply. In verses 24 and 25 we again see the spoken command for the earth to bring forth living creatures, cattle and creeping things and the beast of the earth, followed by the statement that God made all of these.

What are we told about the materials used for various parts of what was created?

Genesis 1:12 says, "And the earth brought forth grass, the herb that yields seed according to its kind, and the tree that yields fruit, whose seed is in itself according to its kind." In Genesis 1:24 we read that God said, "Let the earth bring forth the living creature according to its kind; cattle and creeping things and beast of the earth, each according to its kind." And in Genesis 2:9 we read, "And out of the ground the Lord God made every tree grow that is pleasant to the sight and good for food."

Everything seems to have been made out of the earth or ground, but with two exceptions. In Genesis 2:7 we are told that man was formed of the "dust" of the ground which may mean that carefully selected particles or elements of the earth were used. These thoughts will be explored in more detail later on. Genesis2:21-22, God took a rib from Adam which He then made into a woman. The idea of forming causes me to think of a potter forming a vessel out of a lump of clay. The potter will have a specific design in mind which will depend on its expected use and what it is to look like; he will then very carefully use his hands to form the clay precisely into what he has designed. Likewise, I believe God had specific plans for Adam, so when He took the dust (elements) of the earth He must have very carefully, with His hands, put them together so Adam could fulfill the form and the uses He had designed. "But now, O Lord, You are our Father; we are the clay, and You are our potter; and all we are the work of Your hand" (Isaiah 64:8).

2

THE SEQUENCE

With regard to man, one of the most awesome verses is Genesis1:26. God said, "Let Us make man in Our image, according to Our likeness." God formed man not only to do what He had planned for him, but He also made us to be like Him. We can't grasp what all of that means, but we can be sure we have many of the characteristics of our Father, His Son and the Holy Spirit. He then breathed into his nostrils the breath of life, and man became a living being (2:7). The King James Version of that verse says that man became a living soul, which I believe is more accurate than "living being." Our souls are where we find what makes us into His image: to think, plan, desire, love, rejoice, sorrow, share and forgive, and to know Him. It is our souls that are able to communicate with God and begin an eternal life when we become His.

Genesis 2 records some of the sequence of events. Verses 4-7 tell us no vegetation was on the earth until God sent rain, and no man was there to work the ground. But streams came up and watered the whole surface of the ground, and then God formed man. Verses 8-9 tell that God had planted a garden with all kinds of trees, including the tree of life and the tree of the knowledge of good and evil. Then, in verses 15-17, God put the man in the Garden of Eden to work it and care for it and gave him a warning about not eating from the tree of the knowledge of good and evil. God then said that man needed a helper suitable for him, verse 18. In verses 19-20 Adam had the job of naming all the beasts of the field and the birds, and he did.

But in that process no helper suitable for him was found—not even a monkey or chimpanzee. That day concludes with the making of a suitable helper. God caused

Adam to fall into a deep sleep and performed the first operation on mankind. It must have been a very deep sleep! He took a rib from Adam and made a woman from the rib. Next, God took the woman to Adam. I wonder if he had to wake up Adam since he had been working hard naming all the animals. He might have said, "Please, Lord, let me sleep a while longer." I think, though, when he saw Eve he was satisfied that God had made a help-meet suitable for him. He might have even uttered a WOW or two. I hope Eve was also happy with this guy with whom she would spend the rest of her life. And so Adam was able to name the one that was suitable for a helper. He named her Woman.

Let me explain why I have been interested for some time in putting together some thoughts about the process of creation. I have, on occasion, gone to one of my favorite spots by the St. Clair River to enjoy the view, along with the peace and quiet there. While sitting there I have contemplated the magnificence God has created for our enjoyment and wondered how it all came about. Too often we neglect to think, beyond the statements in His

Word, about the actual processes involved. As we think about the details of creating the heavens and the earth, the grass and trees, fish and birds, animals, and finally man and woman we can get a better grasp on the wonder of our magnificent God who designed and made it all. So I hope you will join me in speculating about some of the details and contemplating the awesome power of God evident in His love for us by providing the beauty of all that is around us.

QUESTION: What existed prior to the creation of the heavens and the earth?

Chapter 8 of Proverbs may add something to help us think about the process of creation. This chapter is about wisdom and understanding. In verses 22-23 we are told, "The Lord possessed me (wisdom) at the beginning of His way, before His works of old. I (wisdom) have been established from everlasting, from the beginning, before there ever was an earth." Verse 25 continues: "Before the mountains were settled, before the hills, I (wisdom) was brought forth while as yet He had not made the earth or the fields, or the primal dust of the world." So God clearly used wisdom and understanding before He began the actual process of creating.

Before God began forming man and woman He must have done a lot of designing; not only did He create a living, breathing couple, but He designed them to be compatible physically, emotionally and spiritually; He designed them so they would bring about others just like them. He did not have to form other men and women to fill the earth—He passed that privilege to Adam and Eve. In Genesis 2:24 we find the statement, "For this reason a man will leave his father and mother and be united to his wife, and they will become one flesh." I believe this includes being of one mind, having one desire for most of what life brings to them. Not that we won't have differences of opinion occasionally or frequently—I don't even agree with myself from morning to evening sometimes—but that we essentially agree about things that matter.

The apostle Peter in his letter to believers tells them they were redeemed by the blood of Christ who was foreordained before the foundation of the world (1 Peter 1:18-20). *So, through the wisdom that existed before creation was begun, God had planned the way for mankind to be reconciled to Himself through the sacrifice of His Son.*

3

THE PRIMAL DUST

*W*hat was the "primal dust" composed of that He formed into the first living, breathing man? What were the elements of which Adam was made? Since God took the "dust (elements) of the ground" when He created (formed) man we might wonder how those elements got there. We are not given much detail about the makeup of the earth God created. But the Word tells us the Spirit of God hovered over the face of the waters (Genesis 1:2). Also, in Genesis 1:6 we are told God put a firmament in the midst of the waters, so the elements of hydrogen and oxygen must have been present in that water. Since scientists identify at least twelve other elements as being essential in humans, we have to assume that when God created the heavens and the earth all of these elements were a part of creation. This should make us stop and think about the complicated process of creation.

Obviously, when God took the elements He had already made a part of the earth, He still had the process of forming them into man. Can you imagine the process of taking these elements and forming skin or an artery, a fingernail, a heart, brain cells, an eye? The list goes on. Consider the design of the heart that would send blood down to the big toe and back again, the structure of brain cells that would allow a person to think, to recognize his mother. That's another mystery.

Dr. David Jeremiah, in his *Turning Points* devotional for October 29-30, 2016, mentions these facts: One hundred thousand miles of blood vessels. The ability to remember fifty thousand aromas. Unique fingerprints and tongue prints. Ability to distinguish between different colors. Eyes with the equivalent of 576 megapixels. Four pounds of bacteria; more bacteria in your mouth alone than people in the world.

The more we learn about our bodies the more we are amazed at the designing and planning God must have done before He even started the creation process.

Let's look at the elements that make up the human body. In "Elements in the Human Body and What They Do," an article on the Science Notes website (sciencenotes.org), Dr. Anne Helmenstein gives these facts: Six elements make up ninety-nine percent of the body, and another five are most of the final one percent. The most abundant element is oxygen—about sixty-five percent. Most of that is part of the water in the body, but another function is to supply the lungs and bloodstream for the cells and tissues of the body. The second most prevalent element is carbon; every organic molecule of the body contains carbon. Third is nitrogen, and fourth is calcium. Although most of the calcium is found in bones and teeth, its most important use is in muscle contraction and regulation of protein. Another important element is potassium. Although it accounts for only one quarter of one percent of the body mass, it is critical for nerve conduction and regulating the heartbeat.

Scientists and doctors tell us many elements are part of our bodies and, in many cases, too much or too little of them can drastically affect our health. We are aware that calcium, carbon, sodium and iron are some of the elements that doctors carefully monitor when we develop difficulties of various types. Scientists tell us many elements are necessary for good health and traces of as many as sixty elements can be found in our bodies.

Have you ever made (created) anything from LEGOs? People have made fantastic things using LEGOs: buildings, even whole villages, animals (not living), vehicles and many other objects. But I doubt that you had to create the LEGOs you used. Or maybe you built things using an Erector set, but I don't expect that you were able to make the pieces yourself. In the same way, God had to first create all the elements from which everything else was made. If a friend told us he formed (made, created) a car from whatever happened to be handy, we would have tons of questions about the process, such as where did he find the parts, who made them and put them there, how did he know how to put them together, and did he really do it?

Since the human body, according to scientists, contains so many chemical elements, it seems reasonable to wonder where these elements came from. We might speculate about the original act of creation when God created the earth that the formless, empty ball contained every chemical element: electrons, protons, neutrons, the atoms from which everything in the universe was made. *The heavens and the earth came not from anything already there but simply from the power of God who made it all.*

Likewise, we are not told about the condition of the heavens, but we know it wasn't until the fourth day that the sun, moon and stars were formed. As we try to imagine the process of making all the stars in the universe and setting them in the paths they would follow we are faced with a total lack of comprehension. The wisdom and power of our God to design and create the universe around us has to create in us, not just awe about all of it. But He also must create in us an understanding that He is able to care for us, as He tells us in His Word, and to keep us until the day when we will see Him face-to-face.

4

THE BEAUTY OF NATURE

*D*uring the third day of creation God spoke, and the earth brought forth grass, herbs and trees that produce fruit as well as seed that assured a continuing growth (Genesis 1:11-12). These were to continue "according to its kind," which indicates the presence of many varieties. The earth was being stocked with sources of food, but we are not told the reason for this abundance of food until the creating continues on the fifth day. Then God spoke, and the earth became inhabited by great sea creatures and all the things that lived in the waters and every winged bird. All of these were created after their kind. We shouldn't be surprised then that scientists today are able to identify astounding numbers of kinds of sea creatures and birds. They have indeed been fruitful and multiplied according to His command.

The fourth day of creation set the stage for the beauty and practicality of an astounding array of lights with which we are blessed: the lights that separate the day from the night and lights that separate seasons, days and years. God made two great lights that we know as the sun and moon. He also made the stars that fill the heavens and fill us with awe as we contemplate the greatness of the universe that surrounds us. And God saw it was good. And so the universe continued to be prepared for mankind.

On the sixth day of creation God brought forth by His command living creatures of every type: cattle, beasts, creeping things, each according to its kind. Again we are left in absolute awe as we contemplate the magnitude of creation. If we think about the design of just one animal — the elements it's composed of, the fact that it is a living thing and our inability to accomplish anything remotely similar — we must get a fleeting idea of what God has made and His incredible power. Then God said, "Let us make man in our image." So God created man in His own image—male and female He created them. He blessed them with the instructions to be fruitful, to fill the earth and subdue it, and to rule over all the living creatures. And God saw it was very good.

The awesomeness of realizing every little particle created was designed to make lights in the heavens, animals, fish and birds, grass, trees, fruit, seeds and finally man is far beyond our ability to comprehend. What do these thoughts tell us about God? Should it surprise us we are told in His Word that He knew us before we were born, (Psalm 139:13, 15-16)He knows our coming and our going, (Psalm 139:7-10) He understands our needs, (Philippians 4:19) and He has made it possible for us to spend eternity in His presence? (John 14:2-3)

"By the word of the Lord the heavens were made, and all the host of them by the breath of His mouth. He gathers the waters of the sea together as a heap; He lays up the deep in storehouses. Let all the earth fear the Lord; let all the inhabitants of the world stand in awe of Him.

For He spoke, and it was done; He commanded, and it stood fast" (Psalm 33:6-9).

And "who has measured the waters in the hollow of His hand, measured heaven with a span and calculated the dust of the earth in a measure? Weighed the mountains in scales and the hills in a balance? Have you not known? Have you not heard? Has it not been told you from the beginning? Have you not understood from the foundations of the earth? It is He who sits above the circle of the earth, and its inhabitants are like grasshoppers, who stretches out the heavens like a curtain, and spreads them out like a tent to dwell in. Lift up your eyes on high, and see who has created these things, who brings out their host by number; He calls them all by name, by the greatness of His might and the strength of His power; not one is missing" (Isaiah 40:12-13, 21-22, 26).

As I sit here listening to beautiful music playing on the radio, I wonder if God had created only one tone for sound, or if our ears were able to detect only one tone, if all the trumpets my son plays sounded only one note, what would the world be like? What if He had created only one color? How would you like a black-and-white world? What if He had created only one fruit and one vegetable? Would you like a steady diet of apples and broccoli? As we enjoy the world around us do we thank God for the beauty of His handiwork? If every person looked identical (I hope not like me), how would you have picked your husband or wife? God, in His design of creation, has provided us with an unfathomable variety of things to enjoy.

Today I took a mid-October trip to one of my favorite places; the trees were just beginning to take on their fall colors. As God designed the trees it probably was not necessary to make them be transformed every fall into a beautiful display of colors that takes our breath away, but I'm sure glad He did. How often do we consider the wisdom and understanding behind the process of creation, the awesomeness of His love for us in providing all of this and our ability to love, to care and to share it all with each other?

5

CREATION CONTINUES

$\mathcal{P}$salm 104 contains many statements verifying that God is continuing acts of creation. "He sends the springs into the valleys; they flow among the hills. They give drink to every beast of the field. . . . He waters the hills; He causes the grass to grow for the cattle, and vegetation for the service of man. . . . You send forth Your Spirit, they are created. And You renew the face of the earth. . . . He looks on the earth, and it trembles; He touches the hills and they smoke" (Psalm 104: 10, 13, 30, 32). Clearly, although these verses may not relate to what we usually think of as creating, they do tell us about His continuing hand in what happens on the earth. ASSIGNMENT: Read all of Psalm 104.

Isaiah 41:17-20 shows His continuing hand in what happens even today. "The poor and needy seek water, but there is none, their tongues fail for thirst. I, the Lord, will hear them; I, the God of Israel, will not forsake them. I will open rivers in desolate heights, and fountains in the midst of the valleys; I will make the wilderness a pool of water, and the dry land springs of water. I will plant in the wilderness the cedar and the acacia tree, the myrtle and the oil tree; I will set in the desert the cypress tree and the pine and the box tree together, that they may see and know, and consider and understand together, that the hand of the Lord has done this, and the Holy One of Israel has created it."

References to the new heavens and new earth that will be created are found in Isaiah 65:17-25: "For, behold, I create new heavens and a new earth; and the former shall not be remembered or come to mind. But be glad and rejoice forever in what I create; for, behold, I create Jerusalem as a rejoicing, and her people a joy." And in

Isaiah 66:22 we read, "For as the new heavens and the new earth which I will make shall remain before Me, so shall your descendants and your name remain."

In the New Testament we also find references. "But the day of the Lord will come as a thief in the night, in which the heavens will pass away with a great noise, and the elements will melt with fervent heat; both the earth and the works in it will be burned up. . . . Nevertheless we, according to His promise, look for new heavens and a new earth in which righteousness dwells" (2 Peter 3:10, 13). I am confused as to why the heavens will pass away, but I believe since the earth has been changed through sin it will be remade to put it in the original condition God designed.

Also, in Matthew 25:31-34 Jesus tells His followers about when He will come in His glory and sit on the throne of His glory. He will separate the sheep from the goats and then will say to the sheep, "Come, you blessed of My Father, inherit the kingdom prepared for you from the foundation of the world."

In Revelation 21:1-2 the apostle John tells of his seeing the holy city, the New Jerusalem, coming down out of heaven from God, prepared as a bride for her husband. Then in verses 9-27 he records that the angel showed him the holy Jerusalem and gives us the fantastic description of that great city. So, evidently, at least this part of the coming kingdom has been prepared for us back when the world was created.

In Revelation 22:1-2 he describes some of what is inside the city: God's throne, the river of water and the tree of life, bearing twelve fruits. John is shown the throne in heaven and the twenty-four elders worshipping Him saying, "You are worthy, O Lord, to receive glory and honor and power; for You created all things, and by Your will they exist and were created" (Revelation 4:11).

6

JESUS CHRIST, CREATOR

O ne of the most interesting parts of the continuing creation is found in Ephesians 4:22 and 24. "Put off, concerning your former conduct, the old man. . .and put on the new man which was created according to God, in true righteousness and holiness." When we become believers a new person is created in us. This is confirmed in Ephesians 2:10: "For we are His workmanship, created in Christ Jesus for good works." This verse is one of those that show that Christ Jesus was, and is, involved in the creation of everything. John 1:1-4 tells us, "In the begin-ning was the Word, and the Word was with God, and the

Word was God. He was in the beginning with God. All things were made through Him, and without Him nothing was made that was made. In Him was life, and the life was the light of men." Verses 10 and 12 continue, "He was in the world, and the world was made through Him, and the world did not know Him. . . . But as many as receive Him, to them He gave the right to become children of God, to those who believe in His name."

Psalm 103:11-14 contains some very good news for those who believe in Him. "For as the heavens are high above the earth, so great is His mercy toward those who fear Him; as far as the east is from the west, so far has He removed our transgressions from us. As a father pities his children, so the Lord pities those who fear Him. *For He knows our frame; He remembers that we are dust"* (italics added). As God the Father along with His Son Jesus created us, they remember our humble beginnings and have compassion on us.

Such a simple solution to our problems: belief that Jesus, together with God the Father, created the world and all that is in it, belief that He died to take the penalty for our sins, and eternal life is ours through Him. How can we not accept His offer of becoming a new person, beginning a new life and realizing we now belong to the One who made the world and made us in His likeness?

Colossians 1:15-17 confirms that Christ was a partner with God the Father in creating. "He is the image of the invisible God, the firstborn over all creation. For by Him all things were created that are in heaven and that are on earth, visible and invisible, whether thrones or dominions or principalities or powers. All things were created through Him and for Him. And He is before all things, and in Him all things consist." Or, "in Him everything holds together" (NIV). He sustains and controls everything: the earth, the heavens and the laws of nature that keep the stars and the planets in their proper orbits.

One of the most comforting statements Jesus made is found in John 14:2-3. "In My Father's house are many mansions; if it were not so, I would have told you. I go to prepare a place for you. And if I go and prepare a place for you, I will come again and receive you to Myself that where I am, there you may be also." Not only will we have a place in heaven, we will also have new bodies. First Corinthians 15:53-54 tells us we shall all be changed, the dead will be raised incorruptible, and our mortal bodies will put on immortality.

As we reflect on God's wisdom and power by which He created all we see in the heavens and all we can experience on this awesome earth, as we think of what He has created in us by which we can know Him, love Him and serve Him, and what He has promised us for eternity, our minds are incapable of absorbing a complete understanding of Him. And when we realize what He has done through His Son to save the soul He created in us from the power of sin, we are overwhelmed by His Infinite love.

Dear Friend, I pray that these thoughts about creation have stirred your interest in our incredible God and the universe He has created for us to enjoy. If you do not yet know Him and His Son, who died to pay the penalty for your sin, may you today begin seeking for the salvation that was in His plans before the universe began and is free to all who ask.

CPSIA information can be obtained
at www.ICGtesting.com
Printed in the USA
LVOW13s0404300617
539722LV00005B/7/P

9 781498 498869